CRYSTALS

By Rebecca E. Hirsch

Content Consultant
Dave Witter
Adjunct Professor
Materials Science and Engineering
Clemson University

Core Library

An Imprint of Abdo Publishing
www.abdopublishing.com

www.abdopublishing.com

Published by Abdo Publishing, a division of ABDO, PO Box 398166, Minneapolis, Minnesota 55439. Copyright © 2015 by Abdo Consulting Group, Inc. International copyrights reserved in all countries. No part of this book may be reproduced in any form without written permission from the publisher. Core Library™ is a trademark and logo of Abdo Publishing.

Printed in the United States of America, North Mankato, Minnesota
042014
092014

THIS BOOK CONTAINS
RECYCLED MATERIALS

Cover Photo: Marcel Jancovic/Shutterstock Images
Interior Photos: Marcel Jancovic/Shutterstock Images, 1; Shutterstock Images, 4, 10, 17 (upper left), 17 (upper middle), 17 upper (right), 17 (lower middle), 19, 43; Alexander Raths/Shutterstock Images, 7; imagebroker/SuperStock, 9; Nastya Pirieva/Shutterstock Images, 12, 45; iStockphoto/Thinkstock, 15, 21, 36 (Photos 1–5, 7–10), 42 (top), 42 (bottom); Marcel Clemens/Shutterstock Images, 17 (lower left); Karol Kozlowski/Shutterstock Images, 17 (lower right); Kyodo/AP Images, 23; Eye Ubiquitous/Glow Images, 24; Dane Penland/Smithsonian Institute/AP Images, 27; John Cancalosi/age fotostock/SuperStock, 29; Dave King/DK Images, 31; Photodisc/Thinkstock, 35; Hemera/Thinkstock, 36 (Photo 6); Visuals Unlimited/Corbis, 38; Eleanor Bentall/Corbis, 40

Editor: Mirella Miller
Series Designer: Becky Daum

Library of Congress Control Number: 2014932342

Cataloging-in-Publication Data
Hirsch, Rebecca E.
  Crystals / Rebecca E. Hirsch.
    p. cm. -- (Rocks and minerals)
Includes bibliographical references and index.
ISBN 978-1-62403-384-1
1. Crystals--Juvenile literature. 2. Mineralogy--Juvenile literature.   I. Title.
549--dc23

                                                            2014932342

CONTENTS

CHAPTER ONE

WHAT IS A CRYSTAL?

Next time you are outside, look around for a pebble. Pick the pebble up and look at it closely. Do you see any colored flecks? The colors you see are minerals. Minerals are solid substances that form in nature. You use minerals every day. Fluoride in toothpaste and salt found in food are minerals. Minerals are also found in aluminum cans, cell phones, and water.

Many crystals are beautiful, and people use them to make jewelry and other delicate objects.

Most minerals form as crystals. Crystals are hard minerals that appear colorless or colored. They have many edges with smooth surfaces called faces, or facets. These edges form geometric shapes, such as cubes. Crystals can be larger than a school bus or smaller than a speck of dust. Metals such as copper, gold, and silver are also considered crystals.

Understanding Atoms

To better understand crystals, it is important to first learn about atoms. Atoms are the building blocks of the universe. They are small particles that make up everything

How Snowflakes Form

Snowflakes are crystals that form high in the clouds. A cold droplet of water freezes onto a speck of dust. This forms a crystal. As the crystal falls, more water vapor freezes onto it, and the snowflake grows. At other points along its path, the snowflake shrinks. The snowflake continues to grow, shrink, and change shape as it falls. Because each snowflake follows its own path, no two snowflakes are identical. It is possible for two snowflakes to look similar, however.

Scientists study crystals' facets to better categorize their shapes.

around you. The earth, the air you breathe, and all living things are made up of atoms. Atoms are so small that lining up 1 million atoms in a row would be as thick as one human hair.

There are approximately 90 different types of atoms in the universe. They are called elements. Elements cannot be broken down into simpler substances. Oxygen, helium, and gold are examples of elements.

Some minerals are also elements. They are made up of one type of atom. Other minerals are made of a few different types of atoms bonded, or joined, together. This is called a compound. Water is a compound made from hydrogen and oxygen atoms. Salt is a compound made up of sodium and chlorine atoms.

From Atoms to Crystals

Looking through an electron microscope at the inside of a crystal, scientists can see atoms form a pattern. The pattern repeats over and over. In some minerals, such as salt, the sodium and chloride atoms form a cubic pattern.

Some machines create man-made snow crystals by freezing water.

Amethyst, a type of quartz crystal, has a hexagonal shape formed from the pattern of its atoms.

In other minerals, such as quartz, the pattern will be hexagonal. The pattern of atoms can determine the shape of the crystal.

Remember those flecks in the pebble? As the pattern of atoms repeats itself, the crystal fleck will grow larger. When the pattern is repeated many times as the crystal grows, a large crystal forms.

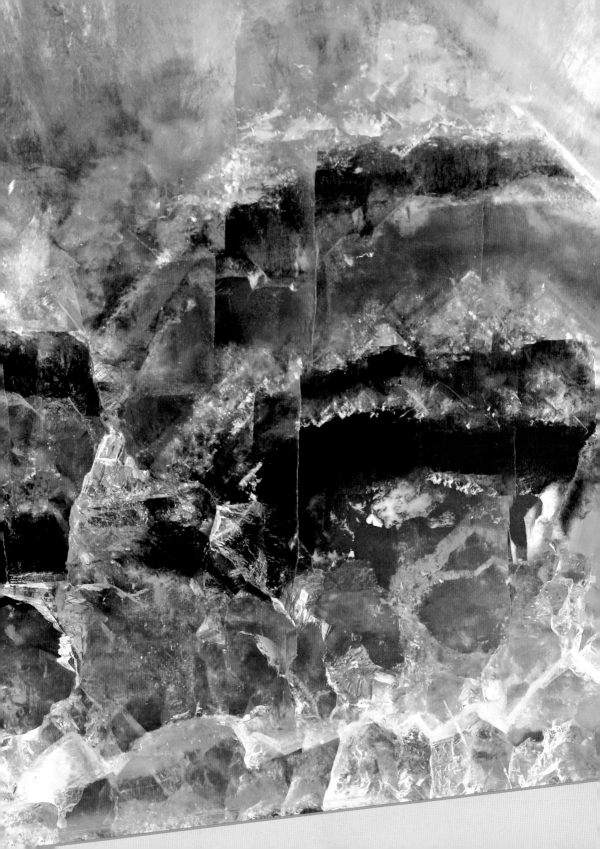

CHAPTER TWO

CRYSTAL SHAPES

C rystals take on many shapes and patterns. If a crystal were cut through its center, its two halves would be mirror images of each other. This is called symmetry. All crystals have symmetry due to the pattern of their atoms. The atoms also give crystals their unique shapes and properties.

Cutting a crystal through its center reveals the pattern of its atoms.

Crystal shapes fall into six main groups based on symmetry. The different symmetries are called crystal systems.

The simplest and most common crystal shape is the cube. Cubic crystals have six square faces. The sides are the same lengths and meet at right angles. A cubic crystal can be cut in half nine different ways, and the two pieces will be symmetrical mirror images. Many minerals, including salt, copper, gold, silver, iron, garnet, and diamond, form into cubes.

The other five crystal systems include hexagonal, tetragonal, orthorhombic, monoclinic, and triclinic. Hexagonal crystals have six sides. Three of these sides are equal in length, while the other three sides are longer or shorter in length. Apatite, beryl, and emerald all have hexagonal crystal systems.

Tetragonal is the least common of all the crystal systems. Tetragonal crystals look similar to square prisms. These crystals can be cut in half five ways,

Yellow fluorite is a mineral that forms into a cubic crystal shape.

and the two pieces will be symmetrical. Zircon is the gemstone that forms into this shape.

The orthorhombic crystal system has three unequal lines. The lines are at right angles to each other. Orthorhombic crystals are usually small, such as topaz and sulfur.

Monoclinic crystals have tilted faces at each end of the crystal. Each crystal has three unequal lines. Jade and gypsum are examples of monoclinic crystals.

The triclinic crystal system has the least symmetry of all the shapes. All of the sides are different lengths. Triclinic crystals include rhodonite and kyanite. Kyanite is a strong, heat-resistant mineral used in porcelain sinks, dentures, and spark plugs.

Growing Crystals

Crystals grow by adding more layers of atoms to their outsides. Tiny crystals can form in minutes. Big crystals take thousands of years to grow.

Many crystals form in water. Crystals grow in liquid solutions when the liquid becomes saturated

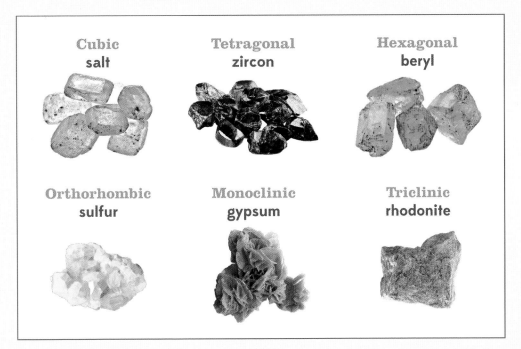

| Cubic | Tetragonal | Hexagonal |
| salt | zircon | beryl |

| Orthorhombic | Monoclinic | Triclinic |
| sulfur | gypsum | rhodonite |

Crystal Systems

Study this diagram of crystal shapes. How does the information compare with what you have learned from Chapter Two about crystal symmetry? How do the crystals' appearances change as the numbers of lines increase? How does seeing the shapes help you better understand crystal symmetry?

with mineral compounds. When a liquid has too many minerals, it is soaked, and more minerals cannot dissolve. Some of the dissolved minerals escape from the liquid by forming as small crystals. Cooling the solution usually increases the saturation and grows the crystals larger.

Geodes

A geode is a stone that forms when a gas bubble is trapped in hot volcanic lava. The lava cools and hardens leaving a cavity in the geode. Geodes contain tiny holes called pores. Mineral-rich water soaks through the pores into the cavity. Over thousands of years, the minerals build up inside. They form layers of beautiful crystals. Although geodes look dull on the outside, breaking one open with a hammer will reveal sparkling, colorful crystals.

Not all crystals grow from liquid. Some crystals grow from a vapor, or gas. This is what snowflakes form from. Other crystals form deep in the earth from molten rock. As the melted rock cools and hardens, crystals begin to grow. These crystals form the colored flecks you sometimes see in rocks.

Diamonds are crystals that form under intense pressure. They often form deep in the earth. Diamonds are made up of carbon atoms. The extreme pressure squeezes the carbon atoms into a tiny diamond crystal.

A diamond becomes big enough to see as more atoms are added to the outside of it.

How Diamonds Are Made

Diamonds form under high pressures and temperatures of 2,000 degrees Fahrenheit (1,093°C) or more. Some diamonds form deep in the earth. Others are made when mountains form and rocks are squeezed together. Diamonds can even form when a meteorite crashes on Earth. This is why diamonds can be found near impact sites, such as Meteor Crater in Arizona. Meteorites are rocks from space that sometimes contain tiny diamonds. These diamonds may have formed when the meteorite survived a high-speed collision in space.

Crystals in Nature

A perfectly symmetrical crystal will grow equally on all sides. But most natural crystals do not have a perfect shape. Crystals often grow in cracks in rocks, and their shape becomes smashed. Even when crystals are grown in a laboratory, gravity tugs on the crystals and distorts them. Scientists on the International Space Station have grown almost perfect crystals in zero gravity.

Though not perfect in shape, different crystals grow in specific ways. This is called a crystal's habit.

Diamonds have been found near the 550-foot (168 m) deep impact site of Meteor Crater in Arizona.

Some crystals grow in blocky chunks. Others look like needles. Hematite grows in kidney-shaped blobs. Sulfate crystals resemble clusters of grapes. Gypsum grows in layers, and mica splits into thin sheets.

Human-Made Crystals

Human-made diamonds are also created using technology. Crystal technology has changed the

FURTHER EVIDENCE

There is quite a bit of information in Chapter Two about crystals, their different shapes, and how they grow. What is one of the main points of this chapter? What key evidence supports this point? Go to the article on crystals at the website below. Find a quote from the website that supports the chapter's main point. Does the quote support an existing piece of evidence in the chapter? Or does it add a new one?

Crystal Formation
www.mycorelibrary.com/crystals

world. Some lasers use liquid crystals. The lasers are used to scan bar codes at the grocery store. Special crystals are also used to detect nuclear materials or events. Crystals can be particularly useful in medicine. Three-dimensional imaging and body scan machines use crystals to create clear images for doctors.

The president of Sharp Corporation, a company that creates electronics, introduces a new liquid crystal television in 2008.

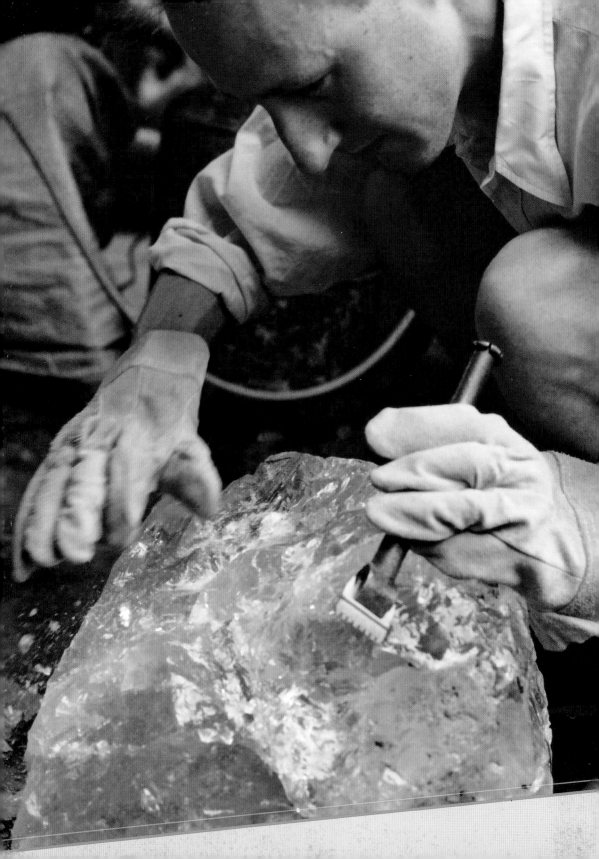

CHAPTER THREE

BEAUTIFUL CRYSTALS

The name crystal comes from the Greek word *krystallos*, meaning "ice." The ancient Greeks thought quartz crystal was ice from deep inside the earth. Now scientists know crystals are made of minerals. When scientists know what minerals make up a crystal, they better understand the type of crystal.

Scientists study crystals to better understand different types of crystals and what they are made of.

Brilliant Colors

Some crystals come in many different colors. Their coloring comes from the minerals they contain. Crystals may also contain impurities, or tiny amounts of other elements or compounds. This changes the color of the crystals. Quartz and sapphire crystals come in a rainbow of colors. Different impurities create the different colors. Rubies are made from the mineral corundum. The red color comes from a tiny bit of chromium mixed in.

Diamonds can be colorless or be one of several colors. These include yellow, brown, orange, blue, pink, or red. The Hope Diamond is a deep blue color. It contains a few boron atoms mixed with carbon atoms. One extra boron atom for every 1 million carbon atoms is enough to create the blue color.

Shiny, Sparkling Crystals

Some crystals glint and sparkle. Other crystals do not sparkle at all. The amount of sparkle depends on the

The Hope Diamond is housed at the Smithsonian Institution in Washington, DC.

type of mineral within the crystal. It also depends on how the crystal's atoms are arranged.

Crystals that allow light to pass through are called transparent. Crystals that do not allow light to flow through are called opaque. Metal crystals such as copper, gold, and silver are opaque.

Crystals also have different types of luster. Luster depends on how light reflects off the crystal's surface. Many crystals, particularly diamonds, look glassy. Other crystals look shiny, while still others look similar to a pearl. There are even some crystals that look similar to satin.

The Hope Diamond

The famous Hope Diamond has a long and mysterious past. In 1668 a 112-carat blue diamond was sold to King Louis XIV of France. The diamond soon disappeared. It surfaced 20 years later in England. It is believed Britain's King George IV bought the gem. It changed owners several more times. One owner kept the famous blue diamond hidden under his couch cushions. In 1958 the gem was donated to the Smithsonian Institution by Henry Philip Hope's family. Hope had been the most recent owner of the gem.

Fluorescence

Some crystals have the appearance of one color in daylight and a different color under ultraviolet light, or black light. This is called fluorescence. The word comes from the mineral fluorite. In daylight fluorite can be purple, yellow, green, or pink. Under ultraviolet light it glows bright blue or green.

Dazzling Gems

Gemstones are rare crystals. They are prized

Willemite is a crystal with a green fluorescence.

for beauty and durability. Gemstones often sparkle with a bright color. Of the more than 4,000 known minerals, only 100 are considered gemstones. The most valuable gemstones are diamonds, emeralds, rubies, and sapphires.

Gemstones are made deep in the earth. They may be pushed to the surface when mountains are made. People may also dig to find gems and other valuable

The Cave of Crystals

Mexico's Cueva de los Cristales, or Cave of Crystals, is filled with enormous crystals. Giant gypsum beams stick out from the walls and the floor. Some of the crystals are longer than a school bus. These giant crystals grew from the gypsum-rich waters that filled the warm 136 degrees Fahrenheit (58°C) cave previously. The crystals were discovered in the year 2000 after a mining company drained the cave for its mining operations.

crystals. To find diamonds, people usually have to dig very deep in the ground.

A gemstone often starts out looking like a dull rock. It must be prepared to make it look beautiful. Opaque stones are rounded and polished. Transparent gems are cut and polished. The gem is glued down to a surface. Then a rough wheel grinds flat faces onto the gemstone at precise angles. Each cut reflects light and shows off the sparkling interior of the gem. Another wheel then polishes the gem.

The Cave of Crystals was discovered in 2000. A *National Geographic* article explains why returning the cave to its natural state by filling it with water may be beneficial:

> In the two-story-tall, football-field-size Cave of Crystals, enormous beams of gypsum—among the largest freestanding crystals in the world—sprout haphazardly from the ceiling, floor, and walls. . . .
>
> "I don't think they'll ever be able to preserve those caves," Miami University's [John] Rakovan said. "It'll be economically unfeasible."
>
> But shutting down the caves isn't necessarily a bad thing, Rakovan added. "It might actually preserve the crystals. And if at a later date it becomes important to get in there again, they could repump."
>
> Source: Ker Than. "Giant Crystal Caves Yield New 'Ice Palace,' More."
> National Geographic. *National Geographic Society*, October 7, 2010. Web.
> Accessed February 11, 2014.

Changing Minds

Take a position on pumping water back into the Cave of Crystals. Imagine your best friend has the opposite opinion. Write a blog post trying to change your friend's mind. Make sure you explain your opinion and your reasons for it. Include facts and details that support your reasons.

CHAPTER FOUR

PUTTING CRYSTALS TO THE TEST

It can be tricky to learn an unknown crystal's identity. Scientists study the color and the habit to learn more about a crystal. They also perform a few other simple tests to get more clues.

Some tests can harm crystals, however. Scientists never perform any of their tests with gemstones that may be worth a lot of money. First they test broken and damaged crystals.

Tests help scientists know what minerals make up a crystal.

Human-Made Gemstones

Rubies, sapphires, emeralds, and diamonds are usually made deep in the earth. But they can also be made in a laboratory. Lab-made gemstones can be tougher than natural ones. And they are used in many different ways. Sapphires are used in supermarket scanners. Rubies are used in tools that help remove tattoos. Some dentists even use diamond-tipped drills to fill cavities.

Up to Scratch

One of the most useful clues when testing a crystal is hardness. A crystal may be as soft as powder. Or it could be as hard as a diamond. Other crystals have a medium hardness.

German scientist Friedrich Mohs invented a scale to measure hardness. Ten minerals are arranged from one to ten on his scale. One is the softest mineral, while ten is the hardest mineral. Talc has a hardness of one and can be scratched by most anything. Quartz has a hardness of seven and is tough to scratch. Diamond has a hardness of ten and cannot be scratched. It can scratch anything, however.

Crystals are used in many everyday objects, including grocery store scanners.

Imagine you are trying to figure out the hardness of a mystery crystal. The easiest way to test a crystal's hardness is to rub it with your fingernail, which has a hardness of 2.5. Next try using a copper penny. It has a hardness of 3.5. Then try using a piece of glass with a hardness of 5.5. Do any of the materials scratch the crystal? If they do, the crystal is softer than the material that scratched it. Or does the crystal scratch any of the materials? If it does, that means the crystal has a higher hardness.

With this information, rank your crystal on the Mohs scale. Let's say your crystal scratches your fingernail and a penny, but it will not scratch glass. This means your crystal has a hardness of approximately 4 or 5. It could be fluorite, which has a hardness of 4, or apatite, which has a hardness of 5.

The Streak Test

Another way to determine what kind of crystal you have is to find out what color it makes when crushed into a powder. The streak test will reveal the answer.

MINERAL		MOHS HARDNESS
Talc		1
Gypsum		2
Calcite		3
Fluorite		4
Apatite		5
Feldspar		6
Quartz		7
Topaz		8
Corundum		9
Diamond		10

The Mohs Scale of Hardness

This chart shows the Mohs scale of hardness. Look at the chart. Let's say you found a red crystal and wanted to find out what it was. How would you use the Mohs scale to test it? Try scratching the crystal with a penny. What happens? Write a paragraph describing how you would test the crystal and what results you find.

The color of the crystal and the color of the streak may not match, as with hematite.

Choose a rough or broken piece of a crystal. Rub it across an unglazed ceramic tile. The crystal will leave a colored streak behind. What color do you see?

You may think a blue crystal will make a blue streak, and so forth. This is true for some crystals. But some crystals surprise you. A calcite crystal can be any color of the rainbow, but it always leaves a white streak. Yellow pyrite leaves a greenish-black streak.

Final Tests

A few other tests can help determine a crystal's identity. One clue is density. Density is the amount of mass squeezed into a given volume. Density is measured using specific gravity. Most rocks have a specific gravity between two and three.

To find out your crystal's specific gravity, bounce the crystal in your hand. Does it feel as heavy as similar-sized rocks? If so, it probably has a specific gravity between two and three. If it feels heavier, it could be galena. This lead ore has a specific gravity of 7.5. If your crystal is really heavy, it could be gold. Some types of gold can have a specific gravity up to 20.

Crystal Skulls

Crystal skulls are carved from transparent or milky quartz. They sit in many museums. Scholars once thought Aztecs made these objects. But now many scholars believe the skulls are fake. Crystal skulls do not look similar to anything from Aztec culture. And no crystal skulls have ever been found at an official Aztec archaeological dig.

Students test limestone chips in hydrochloric acid.

Another test scientists use on crystals is the acid test. They place a drop of hydrochloric acid on a crystal. If the crystal fizzes, it is made of carbon. The fizzing is caused by carbon dioxide gas. The acid test works on limestone, marble, and calcite.

Finally, scientists test to see if a crystal is magnetic. They place the crystal on a piece of iron to see if it sticks. All of these tests help scientists better understand crystals and their importance in the world today.

Archaeologists compared crystal skulls to objects from 500- to 1,000-year-old archaeological sites in Central America. This article describes their results:

> Under magnification, the cup and beads have the kinds of markings that would come from wood and stone tools. They were shallow and irregular, as you might expect from a piece carved by hand. The skulls, however, had more uniform surface patterns. . . . This suggests the large skulls were carved with modern equipment that would not have been available to the people living long ago, says Jane Walsh, an anthropologist at the Smithsonian Institution.
>
> Further analysis of the quartz in the other skull suggested the rock it was made from came from Madagascar, Europe or Brazil—all very far from the Aztec empire, and not at all connected to the empire by any trade network.

Source: Jennifer Cutraro. "Fakes in the Museum: A Close-up Examination of Crystal Skulls Reveals the True, Recent Origins of These 'Relics.'" Student Science. Society for Science & the Public, June 12, 2008. Web. Accessed February 11, 2014.

What's the Big Idea?

Take a close look at this article. What is the main point? Pick out two details that support this point. What can you tell about crystal skulls based on this article?

EGG-Citing Crystals

You can grow crystals in this experiment. Crush three or four eggshells into small pieces and put them in a bowl. Pour one cup of white vinegar over the eggshells. Any bubbles you see are carbon dioxide gas. Now place the bowl in a warm place. Observe your eggshells every few days. As the vinegar evaporates, crystals of calcium acetate will form. The crystals grow in the shape of popcorn.

Watch the eggshells carefully to see calcium acetate crystals.

Salt vs. Sugar

Can you tell the difference between salt and sugar without tasting? You can tell them apart just by looking. Sprinkle salt onto a piece of black paper and sugar onto another piece of black paper. Look closely at the grains with a magnifying glass. Do you notice any differences? The salt crystals are cube-shaped. Sugar crystals are more like rectangles with pointed ends. The color is also different. Sugar looks clear and sparkly. Salt looks dull and frosted.

Had you noticed a difference between salt and sugar crystals before this experiment?

How many crystal shapes can you create with your marshmallows or candy and toothpicks?

Build a Crystal

You can make models of crystals with toothpicks and a bag of mini marshmallows or small gumdrops. Stick toothpicks into marshmallows to make basic shapes. Build a square or a cube with six sides. When you want to build different shapes, look at a picture of crystal systems for more ideas to try.

Why Do I Care?

You may or may not own fancy gems. But that doesn't mean crystals don't affect your life. How do you use crystals? Are there objects you use or foods you eat that come from crystals? How might your life be different if these things didn't exist? Use your imagination!

Take a Stand

This book discusses crystal skulls. People once thought Aztecs made these skulls. Many experts now believe the skulls are fake. Do you think museums should keep crystal skulls on display? Why or why not? Write a short essay explaining your opinion. Make sure to give reasons for your opinion and facts and details that support those reasons.

You Are There

Imagine you have a chance to go into the Cave of Crystals in Mexico. You put on your protective gear and head underground. Do you like what you see? Do you think the cave should be filled with water again, so the crystals can continue to grow? Or should it be kept dry and open so people can see it?

Say What?

Studying crystals can mean learning a lot of new vocabulary. Find five words in this book that you've never heard or seen before. Use a dictionary to find out what they mean. Then write the meanings in your own words, and use each word in a new sentence.

GLOSSARY

compound
a distinct substance formed by the union of two or more chemical elements

face
any of the flat surfaces that form the boundary of a crystal shape

fluorescence
the giving off of visible light when exposed to ultraviolet light

gemstone
a mineral that can be used in jewelry when cut and polished

impurity
a substance that is mixed in tiny amounts with something else

mineral
solid chemical element or compound that occurs naturally in the form of crystals

opaque
not letting light through; not transparent

saturated
soaked or filled with something to the point where no more can be absorbed or dissolved

symmetry
having equal parts or sides

transparent
transmitting light so that objects lying beyond are entirely visible

LEARN MORE

Books

Harding, Jennie. *Crystals*. East Sussex, UK: Walking Stick Press, 2007.

Symes, R. F., and R. R. Harding. *Eyewitness Crystal & Gem*. New York: DK Publishing, 2007.

Tomecek, Steve. *Everything Rocks and Minerals*. Washington, DC: National Geographic, 2010.

Websites

To learn more about Rocks and Minerals, visit **booklinks.abdopublishing.com**. These links are routinely monitored and updated to provide the most current information available.

Visit **www.mycorelibrary.com** for free additional tools for teachers and students.

INDEX

ABOUT THE AUTHOR

Rebecca Hirsch is a former scientist and the author of dozens of books on science and nature for young readers. She lives in Pennsylvania with her husband, three children, one cat, and a small flock of chickens.